WRITE.
PUBLISH.
LEVERAGE.

*The Self-Publishing Guide to Writing and Publishing a Book
that Impacts, Influences and Creates More Income.*

DENNARD MITCHELL

Write. Publish. Leverage.

Printed in the United States of America

ISBN: 978-0-578-81264-9

NL Publishing

DEDICATION

I dedicate this book to you. The individual who knows that deep down inside, there's a message that needs to be shared with the world. You have permission to unleash it.

FREE WRITING MASTERCLASS

I would like to give you access to a free writing masterclass for purchasing my book. Thank you for your support!

TO DOWNLOAD GO TO:

https://bit.ly/FreeWritingMasterClass

TABLE OF CONTENTS

Chapter 1: Your Purpose and Why for your Book? 1

Chapter 2: Types of Books to Consider 19

Chapter 3: The Writing Planning Phase 27

Chapter 4: The Writing Process 41

Chapter 5: Transcription, Editing, and Formatting 57

Chapter 6: Book Cover Design..75

Chapter 7: Preparing to Launch your Book...............................87

Chapter 8: Publishing 95

Chapter 9: 10 Great Ways to Leverage your Book 103

Resources..111

COMMON BOOK TERMS...113

"If there's a book that you want to read, but it hasn't been written yet, then you must write it."

- Toni Morrison

CHAPTER 1

❧

YOUR PURPOSE AND WHY FOR YOUR BOOK?

C ongratulations on starting your book journey. In this chapter, we'll be discussing the purpose of writing your book, which is a very important ingredient in the success of your book. Whatever you do, please don't skip this part of the process. In addition, it's important you understand why a lot of people never embark on this book writing journey. Knowing this will equip you to avoid pitfalls on your journey. And lastly, why you, the person reading this book right now, deserve to be an author.

Why are you writing a book? What's your purpose for writing your book? This is a very important question that I implore you to ask yourself. Be very clear and succinct on why you decided to write a book. Now, I'll give you a few reasons or examples of why some decide to write a book, and you can choose which one you think is best for you. Keep in mind, you may have a completely different reason, and that's great. The point is for you to have a why.

Personal Goal

Some people decide to write a book because it's a personal goal or accomplishment. I have a great friend, Coach TK, who's a wonderful motivational speaker and consultant. She was in the process of writing her book at the time I was writing this book. As a matter of fact, she sent me a picture of her vision board, and on there, it says that she will become an author. So for TK, it's a personal goal, and it's going to be a major accomplishment.

"A bird doesn't sing because it has an answer; it sings because it has a song."

- *Maya Angelou*

Legacy

For some, writing a book is a way to leave a legacy. Think about it for a moment. This will be something that your kids, grandkids, or even someone around the world you do not even know exists will be reading. They one day will be reading your book or holding it in their hands. It's a way for you to leave a legacy, something that will outlive you. As long as people are going online and reading books and we have access to books or it's on someone's bookshelf, you have the ability to leave a legacy.

Expert Status

What about this one? Sometimes people write a book because they want to get what's called "expert status" on a subject matter. Think about it. You're probably reading and saying to yourself, I would like to write a book on gardening or a book on dogs or sewing, et cetera. You may have a skillset; however, having a book will make you an expert.

Credibility

Credibility is another reason why some decide to write a book. It makes you trustworthy and believable. Now, this was one of the reasons I initially started writing books over 10 years ago. As a public speaker, I wanted to give myself an advantage when I was invited to give presentations. Having a book on a topic that you are speaking on makes the audience more receptive to your message.

"You can't wait for inspiration. You have to go after it with a club."

- Jack London

Make Money

If you're taking notes or making a list, this is number five. How about making money? Yes, it's perfectly okay. You can publish a book to add a new stream of income, and there's absolutely nothing wrong with that. If you're a coach, speaker or consultant, or just want to have an extra stream of income, this is an excellent way to do so.

Promotion

Writing a book is a wonderful way to promote yourself. It is a great tool to display your skills, talents, and expertise. A book is literally like a business card on steroids. It's like having a billboard that you can walk around with. You can carry it with you in your car, backpack or purse. A book is something you can give to people, and when they see it, you will be top on their mind when they need someone with your gifts, talents, abilities.

Media

Number seven, media or press exposure. This is a great way to get media exposure on local as well as national radio and TV outlets. I tried this when launching my book. I decided to distribute a few press releases, and it was amazing because these press releases were blasted locally as well as nationally, lending credibility to me. So when people would Google my name, they would see that I did a book release, and different media outlets were picking up my press release to promote not only the book but also my speaking and consulting services.

"Tears are words that need to be written."

-Paulo Coelho

Speaking Opportunities

You can use your book to secure speaking engagements. Now, this is amazing. You can use your book to get more speaking engagements. If you're someone that's saying, "Hey, I would love to do more speaking, or I would like to add some more dates on my calendar," having a book can definitely help you with that. So as you're sending out your marketing material, you can also send out little snippets of your book to potential clients.

Title "Author"

Now, I don't even have to explain this any further. This is just cool. Think about it for a moment. You get to go around and introduce yourself to people as an author. When someone asks, "what do you do?" You just clear your throat and say, I'm an author. Oh, that just sounds good. I hope you get used to that rolling off your tongue because being an author is an amazing thing. You can add this new title to all of your signatures when you're sending emails. You can add that you are an author on all of your social media profiles, and believe it or not, people will look at you totally different. They will say, "wow, you've written a book. That's something I've always wanted to do," and so now they're going to hold you in high regard all because you have the title of an author. As I said, it's just cool.

Your Story

You have a story. Yes, you have a story. Sharing your story is a chance for people to learn more about you. This is a chance for people to take a piece of you home with them. A chance for you to help someone create a change in their life. A chance to help someone transition from where they are to where they want to be.

"We write to taste life twice, in the moment and in retrospect."

-Anaïs Nin

When my friends and I were graduating from high school, we were trying to figure out what we wanted to do in life. Some of my friends decided that they would go to the military, and some decided they were going to pick up a trade. Some even decided that they would take a year off before deciding what to do with their future.

I decided to go off to college immediately. Now, at the time, I had a dream to be a funeral director/Embalmer. Yes, a funeral director. So what did I do? I did my research, and I enrolled in one of the best schools, Gupton Jones College of Funeral Services, located in Decatur, Georgia. I moved from Miami, Florida, and was living in Atlanta, but I was going to school in Decatur. This experience was something I really enjoyed. This was the first time in my life I was able to make a correlation between everything I was learning and or have learned in high school and everything I was learning in college, and I was able to apply it to a real-life experience. And that's what I was doing in this field.

Now, my goal was to graduate, which I did graduate at the top of my class. I moved back to South Florida a few years later, and here I am, working in the career of my dreams. I am actually doing what I said I was going to do. I'm now an intern funeral director. Every day, I would go to work excited to learn. I was the person who worked in the preparation room. I would help to prepare the bodies for the funeral. And this was a service I felt was much needed. And I felt that I was really helping families at a very vulnerable time in their lives. But then something changed.

I remember going to work one day, and instead of being intrigued about the next thing I was going to learn or the next thing I was going to discover, I started wondering if the individuals I was preparing fully lived. I started asking myself questions like, did this person accomplish all of their dreams and goals? I thought about this often. But I continued to go to work and, and each time I would go to work, I was losing something. I didn't have the same feeling.

"To survive, you must tell stories."

--Umberto Eco, The Island of the Day Before

One day while working, I noticed a trend. The people I was preparing for the funerals started getting younger. In my first year, I noticed many older people came through the funeral home, which saddened me, but I would rationalize, saying that you know what? They lived a long life, and now it's time for them to be at peace and rest. Then I noticed that I would start seeing teenagers and young adults. So then it really started bothering me. I'm like, wait a minute, what am I doing with my life right now? I don't know about you, but have you ever been in a situation where you just felt like there was more to life than what you're doing? Have you ever been in a situation where you just felt like there was a greater calling and purpose on your life?

I had to ask myself, "Dennard, if you were to leave here today, did you accomplish all of your dreams and goals?" And that answer was no. I decided that I was going to leave my profession, something that I was passionate about. I was going to commit my life to ensure that I can work with individuals while they were still living and let them know that they have greatness, that they have brilliance, that they have a gift inside of them, and I was going to do everything possible to make sure that it became a reality.

I shared that brief story as an example of my story that has been changing lives for more than 15 years at the time of this writing. You have a story inside of you, and there's someone that's around you, someone that's in your life or someone that's not even born yet who needs to hear that story. They need your book. Even if that book is on dogs. The world's biggest dog lover is my wife. She needs your book. If it's someone who wants to write a book about gardening or sewing or speaking, or you want to tell your story of how you overcame something, this is your opportunity.

So, in addition to everything I listed, you have something important you need to share with the world. And I believe that's why you need to write a book.

"Writers live twice."

-Natalie Goldberg

Why people don't write a book

Some people don't embark on this journey to start writing a book for various reasons. However, here are a few with the hopes of you avoiding them.

Too hard.

The process, the concept of writing and getting a book published seems like an impossible task. Well, I'm here to tell you, yes, it is hard, and yes, it is difficult. But it is so doable, and it's so possible. And I'm going to show you how to do that.

Don't have the expertise

That's why I'm glad you're reading this book right now because once you're done, you're going to have everything you need—the A to Z on how to write your book and get it published.

Don't know where to start

Now, I'm going to help you with this. I love this story I heard about Will Smith. By the way, this is just a side note for anybody who knows Will Smith; please let him know I would like to meet him. I'm just throwing that out into the world, so make that happen. Just remember, I'm going to help you with this book, so help me meet Will Smith.

So there's this wonderful story that he tells about when his dad had his brother and him build a brick wall. I want you to think about this book process like a beautiful brick wall that we're building. Will explained that for him and his brother to complete the entire wall, they would have to start with one brick.

"To produce a mighty book, you must choose a mighty theme."

-Herman Melville

Brick by brick is how the wall was completed. As we continue to go through this book, that's going to be us laying the brick one at a time, and before you know it, we'll be able to step back and see this beautiful wall—which we will call our book—completed and changing lives. I would like to thank you again because this is a great place to start.

Doubt

People doubt themselves. They say things like, who would want to hear what I have to say? What if no one purchases or reads it? Don't even worry about that. Your job is just to know that you have brilliance and greatness inside of you, and guess what? Your job is just to get the book completed and to release it to the world, and all you're doing is sowing a seed. Eventually, it's going to take root. Eventually, it's going to flourish, and it's going to bloom, and people, we'll come to it. I'll show you how to get people to come to it as well, as we will be talking about marketing in a later chapter.

Too Expensive

No longer is that an excuse for the book writing and publishing process. Yes, you will have to make an investment, but I can promise you it's not super expensive. It's not going to break the bank, and I'm going to show you a lot of affordable ways that you can use to get this process done.

Not famous, or I'm not a celebrity.

Hey, guys, guess what? I'm not famous. I'm not a celebrity, and guess what? Your friends are not worried about that. They just want to support you. Everybody at your local church just wants to support you. Everyone at your school just wants to support you. Everyone you know online just wants to support you. So don't worry about being famous or being a celebrity. You are a friend; you are a mother. You are someone that people look up to. You are a leader, so you have enough information. So don't worry about it.

"Start before you're ready."

- *Steven Pressfield*

Fear

Oh, this is a huge one. I heard that F.E.A.R. is an acronym for false evidence appearing real. Some people really allow fear to stop them. Now I'm not here to debate whether or not fear is real. But let me tell you this, do not allow fear to stop you. You have support. I'm going to help you. I'm going to walk you through this. I'll hold your hand. So do not be afraid. We're not going to let fear stop us from accomplishing our goal to be an author.

The book already exist

Here's one I hear often. Someone has already written a book on the topic you're interested in. Do not worry about that. I am not the only one who has written a book on student success or how to publish a book. And guess what? There's going to be hundreds, if not thousands upon thousands of individuals after me. They will also write a book on student success and how to publish the new way. So no matter what your subject matter or topic is, it is perfectly okay. You just make sure you pick an amazing topic. You make sure you have an amazing book design front and back and spine, and you make sure that inside, you give the best content you possibly can, and you will not have a problem.

Remember, what's your purpose for writing this book? I believe you should write this book because you are enough, and you are amazing. You have a story. Don't forget to avoid the pitfalls of why people don't write a book. I look forward to sharing more information in the next chapter. Let's do it.

" Writing, to me, is simply thinking through my fingers."

— *Isaac Asimov*

CHAPTER 2

TYPES OF BOOKS TO CONSIDER

Welcome back. So far, in chapter 1, we've discussed the purpose of your book. We've also discussed why individuals decide to write a book. It can be for media or credibility; it could be to add an extra stream of income. Lastly, we covered why people don't write books and the pitfalls to avoid.

Now in this chapter, we will discuss the different types of books to consider. It's my job to give you an option of books to choose from to make your writing process much easier. One of the first things you can do is identify whether you would like to write a fiction or a nonfiction book. Now a lot of people decide on fiction books and many on nonfiction; it's completely up to you. But I want to go over a few examples.

So if you remember, in the last chapter, I told you that I wanted to meet Will Smith and that I'm a huge fan. Well, I was listening to an interview by him years ago, and he recommended a book called *The Alchemist*. This is a very popular fiction book. It's not true. It's not real. It didn't happen. But the story is told so well, and the principles in this book are so amazing that this book went on to be a national and international bestseller, translated in multiple languages. So, if you're reading this and saying to yourself you want to launch a career writing fiction books, *The Alchemist* is a great example.

Here are a few options to consider.

Fiction	Nonfiction
Action and adventure	Art/architecture
Alternate history	Autobiography
Anthology	Biography
Chick lit	Business/economics
Children's	Crafts/hobbies
Classic	Cookbook
Comic book	Diary
Coming-of-age	Dictionary
Crime	Encyclopedia
Drama	Guide
Fairytale	Health/fitness

Fantasy	History
Graphic novel	Home and garden
Historical fiction	Humor
Horror	Journal
Mystery	Math
Paranormal romance	Memoir
Picture book	Philosophy
Poetry	Prayer
Political thriller	Religion, spirituality, and new age
Romance	Textbook
Satire	True crime
Science fiction	Review
Short story	Science

Suspense	Self-help
Thriller	Sports and leisure
Western	Travel
Young adult	True crime

Now you're probably saying, okay, I'm not quite ready to write an entire book solely by myself. That's not a problem. I have options for you too. There are book projects called an anthology or a group book. Before I became a solo author, I decided to get some authorship by adding to a book. So I had the opportunity to write a book with a few authors. This was the first book that I actually had a chance to coauthor. This was a book that had 10 contributing authors, and we all wrote one chapter each. We got together, and we created this book. This was my first book project over 10 years ago. Because I liked it so much, I decided to do it again for my second book. As mentioned earlier, I wanted the title of author so I can add more credibility to my name when I go out and speak. Pretty cool. Right now, if you don't want to go that route and you don't want to have a book with nine or eight different authors on it, then you can just write a book with a co-author, find someone you have an affinity with, pick a topic that you guys both agree on and then you can do that.

" Just write every day of your life. Read intensely. Then see what happens. Most of my friends who are put on that diet have very pleasant careers."

— Ray Bradbury

My third book had only myself and a coauthor. It's real simple. These are a few options that I'm giving you. Now, if I must be honest, I want to really help you out right now and give you what I believe are two of the easiest books. If you just want to get a book out right now, these are two of the easiest books you can do and have done immediately. Number one, believe it or not, is a coloring book. Now let's just say you want to speak to the youth. A coloring book is an amazing way to share a simple message while engaging your audience at the same time.

If you are interested in this option, there's a list of resources at the back of this book to look for potential coloring book designers. The second quickest option is a quote book. This is a book filled with quotes from a lot of successful people and original quotes from yourself. You can put it in the book, and it's going to be used as inspiration. So, think about it. You can do a quote for each day, 365 quotes. You can suggest that people read one quote every morning when they awake or before they go to sleep at night for inspiration. They can reflect on each quote and journey about the quote in the same book. So you want to find out all of the legalities about it and learn everything about a quote book. But that is a great option that you have at your disposal. Remember to check the resources in the back of the book for additional information about the different books to consider.

Now that we've laid our foundation, it's time to start ramping it up a little bit. In the next chapter, we're about to get into the pre-writing process. After that, the writing will begin. See you in the next chapter.

" You fail only if you stop writing."

— *Ray Bradbury*

CHAPTER 3

⌘

THE WRITING PLANNING PHASE

Welcome to chapter 3. In this chapter, we will be discussing the writing process planning phase. Now, this process will be an amazing foundation for you to start to formulate thoughts about what the title of your book may be, the types and the names of the chapters, how many chapters, et cetera. So let's get started. Number one, I want you to be able to determine the difference between your reader and your buyer. So when I ask the question, "who is your audience or who is your reader?" that's totally different in some cases from "who will be buying the book?" For example, for one of my books, *Next Level Students Success*, my audience and the person I'm writing for are high school and college students. However, my buyer is their parents, teachers, principals, activities, directors, student life members at colleges as well as superintendents. So, for this process, I want you to determine who will be reading your book. You will want to write your book in a way that your readers can understand it and can receive the message.

Now, if you're writing books for adults, then they are your reader as well as your buyer. But if you're writing books for students—elementary students, middle school students, high school and college students, they're your readers. But the buyers may be their parents. In some cases, we do have students who purchase books, but for the most part, if you're trying to use your books to get more speaking engagements, if you're trying to use your books to get more credibility, if you want to sell your books in bulk, you want to determine your buyer. So number one, who is your audience—your reader? I want you to figure this out because that's who you will be writing for.

"We are all apprentices in a craft where no one ever becomes a master."

— *Ernest Hemingway*

Number two, I want you to determine who's your buyer. If they're the same person, that's perfectly okay. Number three, what's your subject matter? What will you be talking about in the book? Going back to the example I used with my book, *Next Level Student Success*, we established that the readers are the students, and the buyers are the parents, teachers, principals, et cetera. Now, the subject matter is student success. It is very important that I determined that subject matter because I will bring that back up later when we're discussing potential chapter titles for your book. Make a mental note about your subject matter because we will be addressing it in a later chapter.

Writing Outline

When putting together an outline, this is a great time to be thinking about things such as the chapters. How many chapters do you want to have in your book? What are the names and titles of each chapter? Will our chapters have any subtitles or different subsections? To assist you with this process, I've created a writing outline template for you to download.

To Download Your Writing Outline, Visit:

http://bit.ly/WritingOutline

*Note: When typing into your browsers, please type the W and O in capital letters.

Hopefully, you were able to download the outline template. If you have that in front of you, I would like to just go through that with you. So, number one on the course outline says, what's your book's Main topics? I want you to give that some thought.

"Get it down. Take chances. It may be bad, but it's the only way you can do anything really good."

— *William Faulkner*

What's your book's Main topic? If someone was to come up to you right now and say, "Hey, what's this book all about?" What would you tell them? What is the main topic? What is it all about? My book was all about students succeeding or students' success. That's what it's all about. That's the point I want to get across with my book. So what is your book's main topic?

Number two, I would like you to come up with at least 10 questions you feel someone would ask about your main topic. If someone came up to you to say, Hey, what is this? What is that? Who? What, when, and where, as it relates to your topic, think about the top 10 questions you feel someone can ask you about your book's main topic. Now, if you have more than 10 questions, the more questions, the better, but I want you to try to formulate at least 10 questions about your main topic.

Number three. This is where it starts to get a little interesting. From your questions, you can develop titles for your chapters. So think about it for a moment. If you feel someone can come up to you to ask, what's the importance of goal setting? What's the importance of journaling? You see where I'm going with this. So now I can write a chapter all about goal setting and a chapter about journaling as an example.

So, I want you to really think about it. Find a quiet place that you can sit down and really ask yourself those 10 questions. And then, from your questions, you can develop titles or potential titles for your chapters. And don't worry if it changes. That is perfectly okay. But I want you to start to write down and get those thoughts out of your head so you can get this process going.

Number four, as you see on the outline, the answers from your questions will serve as the substance for each chapter. So as you're answering those questions, you are now starting to add meat to the bones of your book. You're starting to add the substance you can expound on when it comes to the writing process.

"A word after a word after a word is power."

— *Margaret Atwood*

Number five. I would like you to note any personal story or stories you heard of that can help you expound on your topic. If you remember from earlier, I shared the story of Will Smith's dad and how he instructed Will and his brother to build a wall. That's a story that while I was putting together this book, I made a note to include in a chapter. Notice when I was talking about the different types of books and talked about The Alchemist, I referenced Will Smith and an interview that I saw. So as you're going through this process, I want you to write down different stories, quotes, statistics, examples, and analogies that you can use.

Wow. You're writing the chapters of your book. Now let's go ahead and refer back to your printout so you can see exactly how the outline will work.

To Download Your Writing Outline, Visit:

http://bit.ly/WritingOutline

*Note: When typing into your browsers, please type the W and O in capital letters.

As you can see on the outline, numbers 1-4 will help you formulate potential chapter titles. So go ahead and write that in. Also, as you see noted, don't worry, your chapter name can change later. It's perfectly okay. Now, as you can see under that, we have the substance. So the answers to the questions about your topic are the substance you can write in to start to add some extra information for each of your chapters. Once you complete that, below, you can write a story, an analogy, a quote, an example, a statistics, something that you can add to help you make your point.

" Words are a lens to focus one's mind."

— *Ayn Rand*

This outlining process is similar to preseason in the NBA or NFL. This is an opportunity to practice before the game, which is the writing. This is what the writing outline is all about.

When it's time to start writing the book, when it's time to finally get in the game, when it's time to show up, now you will have substance—something that you can literally use as a launchpad to help the writing process to be much smoother. So again, number one, what's your book's main topic? Number two, come up with at least 10 questions you feel someone would ask about your topic. Number three, from your questions, develop titles. So I want you to think about it. Go through those questions and pull out the names or pull out different words from those questions you feel would be a great title or start for a title. Number four, the answers from your questions will serve substance for each chapter. Number five, make a note of stories, quotes, statistics, examples, analogies.

Now, a few more things that I want to discuss as it relates to the writing planning phase for the writing process. I want you to start thinking about how many chapters you think you would like to add to the book as well as how many pages you would like the book to be. One of the things you can possibly do is go to your personal library at home and look at the books you have. This would give you an idea if you would like to have a100 page book or a 200-page book, for example. It's completely up to you. As long as you write something down. It can be 10 pages, you have a book, but I want you to write something. Write something down in your notes that you feel comfortable with. So if a hundred pages is something you feel comfortable with, then I want you to write that down in this outline process that you want a book that's at least 100 pages. Make that a goal. Next, I want you to think about what you want the book size to be. Also, in the resource section in the back of this book, I have all of the book sizes and the terminology used sometimes by the printers. Instead of saying book size, they may ask, what's your trim size? So just know when I'm saying book size, I'm using trim size and book size interchangeably.

" Write. Rewrite. When not writing or rewriting, read. I know of no shortcuts."

— *Larry L. King*

So, ask yourself, what book size do you want? I put a list of all of the common book sizes from fiction, children's books, textbooks, nonfiction memoirs in the resources. As an example, I'm in the nonfiction realm, and one of the common sizes that I've decided to choose from is a 6x9 because when I looked at all of the books on my bookshelf, that's the size that felt good in my hand. I have my picture on the front cover of most of my books. I wanted it to be bold and big, and that's a great size because I was using the entire front cover of the book. So ask yourself what size or what trim size you want for your book? Write that down also in your outline. As we're going through this process and as you're writing, I'm going to show you how to work backward to make the writing process a whole lot easier for you.

Writing Best Practices

Number one. Before we get into the writing process, I want you to think about this. I want you to start by setting up your writing environment. Get your writing environment set up. Find a nice place that's comfortable somewhere that once you're there, the distractions are minimum. A place that you can really go to and get locked in and focused.

Number two. Develop writing habits to start. You might start taking notes or you may start pacing in the room or start talking to yourself or even get still and silent before you start writing. Whatever it is, develop a habit to help you get started.

To Download Your Writing Outline, Visit:

http://bit.ly/WritingOutline

*Note: When typing into your browsers, please type the W and O in capital letters.

" All the words I use in my stories can be found in the dictionary—it's just a matter of arranging them into the right sentences."

— *Somerset Maugham*

Number three. Focus on writing your book. Once you start the writing process, only focus on writing.

Number four. Maintain your focus. You have to be disciplined; understand something, it's not difficult, it's discipline. So I want you to be disciplined all the way through and maintain your focus. And if you feel like your focus is starting to wane, go ahead and stop. Take a deep breath if you have to or walk away for a while and then come back. You'll be refreshed and ready to continue.

Number five. Deal with writing distractions. Well, if you notice that there are distractions, eliminate them from the start. When you are ready to write, put your phone on silent, not vibrate, silent. If you have to put your phone in another room so it does not serve as a distraction while you're writing.

Number six, this is important. Start writing your book! I'm excited because we're almost there. In the next chapter, we will be discussing the actual writing process, and I'm going to show you how you can do it the traditional way. And I'm also going to show you some easier ways to get your book from out of your head to paper.

Enjoying this book?

The best way you can thank a fellow author is to leave a review on Amazon! (Pretty pretty please with cherries on top. You are Awesome!)

CHAPTER 4

C/D

THE WRITING PROCESS

Hopefully, by now, you have had a chance to print your outline and fill out all of your questions to assist you with your writing. We will be using your outline in this process. Now, before we get started, I want you to create the mindset of focusing solely on writing. Don't worry about being perfect. Don't worry about trying to get everything completely right. The only thing I want you to focus on is taking the ideas out of your head and putting them down on paper. That's the first step.

Next, I'm going to show you how to reengineer or work backward to make this process easier. For instance, as an example, if you filled out your outline, you should have an idea by now of how many chapters you will like in your book and approximately how many pages you will like in your book. I'll give you an example. You may want a book with 10 chapters and roughly 150 pages. If we're working backward and reengineering this process, that's approximately 15 pages per chapter. Notice that I said approximately because as we're going through the editing and formatting phase, I'm going to show you little suggestions and tricks you can do to fill some space and make up for some of those 15 pages. So don't think you have to write 15 pages of all words right now because we're just saying approximately because when you're talking about a 150-page book, we're still not including the introduction page, the index page, the context page, et cetera.

" Exercise the writing muscle every day, even if it is only a letter, notes, a title list, a character sketch, a journal entry. Writers are like dancers, like athletes. Without that exercise, the muscles seize up."

— *Jane Yolen*

So right now, I just want you to try to break it down into small chunks. And if you have an idea of a 150-page book right now, I want you to focus on 15 pages per chapter. That's what we will be working on. So let's get into the different tools to help you with the writing process. Here's one of the first things you can do to help you along this process. If you're someone that's saying, okay, what is this all about? How do I get the ideas out of my head and put them on paper? Well, the first one I'm going to show you is the traditional model. This is how it's always been done, and for the individuals that are still comfortable with this method, you can use this and that's the old fashioned pulling out your laptop and using a Word document.

Now, depending on which type of computer you're using, it could be a Word document or Pages if you use a Mac book. But this is an opportunity to pull out your laptop and literally open up a Word document or Pages. When I typed up my last book, I typed it on my Mac. So, I was able to find a template that was roughly six by nine, and as I was typing in those templates, I had an idea of how many words per page to get a full page. If you're using a word document, you can change your settings, and you can set your margins so that you can have a template based on your trim size. This is the most traditional way. If you're familiar and comfortable with this, there's nothing wrong with it. You can just pull out a laptop or your desktop and type away.

Next, if you're someone that posts a lot of valuable information on social media, this would be a great idea for you to go back through all of your social media accounts and compile all of the information you've been sending out. If you're someone that sends out a quote of the day with some inspiration. If you're someone that sends out words of encouragement to an individual. If you're someone that sends out articles and advice on a particular subject or field of expertise. If you have a certain niche that you're in, this is your opportunity to go back over all of the years that you've been sending out posts on Twitter, Facebook, Instagram, and LinkedIn, etc. You can use this as a starting point or a template to start your writing process or an idea.

" If you write one story, it may be bad; if you write a hundred, you have the odds in your favor."

— *Edgar Rice Burroughs*

Number three. Just like with the social media post, you can use previous blog posts. If you're someone that blogs a lot, you can use different blog posts that you've sent out in the past, and you can pretty much compile all of those together and literally have a book based on different blogs that you've put out. Now the titles of your blog post can be the potential titles of your chapters. So you have a lot of flexibility there.

Number four. Now, this is one I have never done, but I've read up on it, and it works for some people, but when we're talking about doing something in an affordable fashion, this really does not fit in that category. For those who just do not have the time or do not want to spend that energy towards writing their book, maybe they want to share the ideas, but they don't want to actually sit down and write their book. Then you can hire a ghostwriter. A ghostwriter is someone you can hire to write your book from beginning to end, and they will sign an agreement giving up any rights to the writing. They make their money by writing the book and turning over the rights of the entire manuscript to you. And then you can use that as you see fit. So, if you're interested in taking that route, you can look into that. Just for the sake of this chapter, I decided to add it, but I have not hired a ghostwriter. My book publishing career started over 13 years ago with me going old fashion, using desktops and laptops. I've also gone the route of using past social media posts and blogs.

Number five. You can get a presentation transcribed. If you are a speaker, a consultant, a workshop presenter, you can literally take the recording of your presentations and hire someone to transcribe them in written form. Once they transcribe the recordings to written form, you or someone you hire can organize it in a way that sounds more like writing than speaking.

"...And the day came when the risk to remain tight in a bud was more painful than the risk it took to blossom."

— *Anaïs Nin*

Now, suppose you would like to save money and make that process a little more affordable. In that case, you can hire a friend, ask a family member, a spouse, a boyfriend, a girlfriend if they would like to spend the time and listen to your recording and transcribe it for you, and even help you to format it in a way that it sounds like you're writing a book as opposed to giving a presentation and then you can take that manuscript and send that over to an editor.

Number six. You can speak into a voice recorder on your phone or a voice recorder app. Now, this is something that I really like, and I think this is the way most people are going to start doing books now and even in the future. If you think about it, we all now have great quality cell phones that we walk around with every day. I would recommend that if you have thoughts throughout the day or if you have time set aside throughout the day in which this is book writing time, and you're locked in with no distractions. I recommend that if you're not comfortable with typing everything down on your laptop in a Word document or on your Mac in Pages, use either your iPhone or your Android. You can use the high-quality recorder on there to get all of your thoughts out of your mind and on to the recorder. Then you can listen to them and type them yourself. Or you can record yourself for days and days and then compile all of the recordings, send that over to someone, and they can transcribe that as well. I know I said put cell phones away; however, it will be a tool for you at this point and not a distraction. Suggestion: Keep your phone on airplane mode while recording.

Let's go through that one more time. Number one, you can simply pull out your laptop, or you can go to your desktop, and if you're using a PC, you can do it in a Word document. If you are using the Mac, you can use Pages. Set your margins accordingly or pick a template. Number two, you can comb through all of your social media posts, your Twitter, Facebook, LinkedIn, Instagram. If you've posted any information in the past about encouraging people or giving them suggestions or giving them the

" Know that the Creator lives and moves and breathes within you. So those dreams? Risk them. Those words? Write them. Those hopes? Believe them."

— *Elora Nicole Ramirez*

top 10, 7, or 3 tips. You can compile all of that information and have that put into a book format. Number three, you can go back and look over all past blog posts, and you can use that as well. Number four, you can hire a ghostwriter, someone who would take your thoughts and ideas or a concept, and they will write your book for you from inception to completion. Number five, if you are a speaker, a consultant, a workshop presenter or a teacher—someone who's in front of people all the time—you can literally record yourself giving a presentation or record yourself talking on a particular subject matter or topic and have that transcribed because that will serve as a great starting point. Then you can sit and add to it. Number six, you can speak into a voice recorder on your phone or a voice recorder app. If you're someone that does not have a phone with a voice recorder, you can go to one of your local retail box stores such as Walmart or Best Buy to purchase a digital voice recorder. Or you can buy one off Amazon at a very nominal fee. What you can do is record on that voice recorder, and with its USB port where you can plug it into your computer and download the files to your computer, you can send that over to someone to have it transcribed.

So, now at this point, you will have your book manuscript completed. Now, the only thing we would have to do is get it edited. So those were my six top recommendations as it relates to the actual writing process, taking the ideas out of your head, getting them on paper, or getting them into a voice recorder, getting it transcribed, and then you can have it on paper. So now you can really start seeing the process come to life. Once you have a manuscript in your hand, it now makes that figment of your imagination a reality. And now, all we have to do is continue to go through it, continue to read it, continue to make changes, continue to make edits to it, and then we can now start to see that we have a book.

" Art is not about thinking something up. It is the opposite — getting something down.

— *Julia Cameron, The Artist's Way*

List of Writing Resources

Writing your thoughts and ideas:

1. Voice Recording Apps (REV.com)
2. Voice recorder on your phone
3. Digital voice recorder
4. Laptop
5. Desktop

Getting your recordings transcribed:

1. fiverr.com
2. rev.com
3. upwork.com
4. Friend or family member

Writing Formula

In addition to helping you with the tools for the writing process, I want to help you out with what's called a writing formula. Now, once you put together your book outline, you'll have an idea about how many chapters you want. You'll have an idea about how many pages you want. You'll have an idea about the process and the tools you're going to use for the writing process. Here's a formula that you can use for each chapter to make the process even easier.

It goes like this. Number one, it's your chapter. Identify what's going to be your chapter. So if we're working on chapter number one, what's the name of that chapter?

The writer is an explorer. Every step is an advance into a new land.

— *Ralph Waldo Emerson*

Number two, under your chapter, determine whether or not you're going to have a subcategory or subsection. So you can have multiple categories and sections within that one chapter, which is optional. Remember, as I mentioned before, you can look at all the books in your library at home or go online and look at some of the books present on Amazon. If you have the ability to go to a local bookstore or library, that's great as well. Figure out the chapter, figure out if you would like to have a subcategory or a subsection.

Next, pick a topic or a point that you want to make in that chapter. To support the topic or point, you can tell a story or give an example. If you recall earlier, when filling out your outline, I said if you have any ideas of stories, examples, analogy, statistics, this is where you're going to insert them. So pick a story or an example to support your point and then you expound on that for a while, and then you close your story, example or point out with an action step or how-tos. You give the reader a directive. You tell the reader what you need them to do next. In order to be successful, you need to do one, two, and three. To take your life to the next level, you need to do A, B, and C.

So again, the writing formula is:

1. Pick a chapter.
2. Determine if you will have a subcategory or a subsection under that.
3. Make sure that you have a topic or a point that's going to be the main theme of that chapter
4. Have a story or an example to take your readers on this journey so they can understand the point or topic you want to get across.
5. Support your story with quotes or statistics if necessary.
6. Give them action steps or how to's.

" I am like a little pencil in God's hand. He does the writing. The pencil has nothing to do with it."

— *Mother Teresa*

Now that's a simple formula that you can use for each of your chapters to make the writing process much easier. So if you're reengineering and want a book that's 150 pages with 10 chapters, that's approximately 15 pages per chapter.

You're going to focus on chapter number one with those 15 pages. So do that for chapter number one, 15 pages. Chapter number two, 15 pages. Chapter number three, do 15 pages. If you continue that for each chapter, before you know it, you will have a book with 150 pages, and now we can send a manuscript over to the editors and then get it formatted and before you know it, you will have a book in your hand.

As you can tell, we just literally went through the entire writing process. This is when I need you to focus and tell yourself that for the next week, two weeks, three weeks, you will only focus on nothing else other than getting the book written. You can literally get this writing process done in 30 days or less.

Make sure you complete your outline. Give it the necessary time and attention because once you have an adequate outline, that's going to make this writing process entirely easy. Just determine what's going to be your method of writing, whether it's going to be on a laptop or desktop? Are you going to use social media posts? Are you going to use your blogs? Are you going to hire a ghostwriter? Are you going to get your voice transcribed from a presentation, or are you going to get your voice recordings that you've done at your home? Will you do a combination of methods? Either method will work, but all I'm telling you to do now is take action. You have everything you need as it relates to writing your manuscript. It's writing time!

" Everybody walks past a thousand story ideas every day. The good writers are the ones who see five or six of them. Most people don't see any."

— *Orson Scott*

CHAPTER 5

❦

TRANSCRIPTION, EDITING, AND FORMATTING

Congratulations! We are at the halfway point of this book. So far, we have discussed why you should write a book, the purpose of your book, the different types of books to consider, the writing process planning phase, and the actual writing process. In this chapter, we will be discussing professionally editing and formatting your book at an affordable cost. But before we can do that, hopefully, by now, you have had the time to complete your manuscript. If you did not, this is a great time for you to pause and place a bookmark in this book. Complete the writing phase in its entirety before you move on to the editing process.

Transcription

If you've decided to use a voice recording or a presentation and would like to get that transcribed, we will talk about that now. So, before we talk about the editing and the formatting, let's talk about getting your book transcribed.

The first option I would suggest is you can do it yourself. Now, this is not the easiest way, but this is the most affordable way. So if you have the time and the energy, if you feel this is a skillset that you have, you can literally spin a couple of hours per day going through your presentations or going through your voice recordings and transcribe it the best that you can. Take it from the audio and type it into a word format so that you can send that over to the editor.

Number two, you can have a friend or a family member transcribe your audio for you. Now again, this is not the best option. However, this is an affordable option and if you have a friend or a family member that's willing to put in the time as well as energy and you

" Writing a book is like telling a joke and having to wait 2 years to know whether or not it was funny."

— Alain de Botton

Feel they have the skillset and will give it the necessary attention it needs, then I think that would be a great option for you.

Number three, this is what I recommend, and this is something that I personally have done. I think you should hire a professional at an affordable price. Now, you can check all of your local outlets and what you would be asking for specifically is seeing if you can get someone to do a voice transcription or an audio transcription. But, if you don't want to do the work, I've done the work for you so, I have a recommendation that you can try. It's called hire a freelancer to help you or use a software. You can find someone for hire on sites like UpWork or Fiverr.

On UpWork and Fiverr, you will be able to set up a free account, and you can hire individuals to do the work for you. You have a chance to read their profiles, their reviews that they got from previous clients, and you can make an educated choice on whether or not to invest your money with them. I like UpWork and Fiverr for many reasons. One, it's online, so you now have the ability to work with individuals from all around the world. Number two, the prices are very affordable. You can hire individuals to do a job, from anywhere from five to a hundred dollars, depending on what you need. So using UpWork, Fiverr or sites like it, I believe, is one of the best options there is.

Another great option for transcription is to use Apps like Rev or software like Dragon Naturally Speaking. With this, instead of hiring someone, you can speak directly into your phone or upload your audio and have it transcribed.

" Too many of us are not living our dreams because we are living our fears."

— Les Brown

Editing

Once you have your final manuscript, you are ready to send it over to the editor. And now, before we send anything over to the editor, I would like to just share this with you because it's very important if you are writing or typing up your manuscript on a PC—most editors prefer a Word document, not a PDF. If you are typing your document on a Mac, you may start by doing it in Pages, but convert it to a Word document before sending it to your editor. I just want to save you some time. So just make sure you have it prepared in a Microsoft Word document. Now, it is time to get your book edited.

The same options apply as with the transcription. Number one, this is not the best way, but this is the most affordable way to get your book edited. You can do it yourself. I would only recommend you doing that if this is your skillset.

Number two, have a friend, a family member, or even a teacher do it for you. For my third book, I had a past English teacher from high school edit it. And to be honest with you, that was an amazing process. This process was really affordable because she was willing to do it at no cost because I was a former student, and she was excited and happy for me. So, that's an option for you. Check with a friend you know, a spouse, a family member, a teacher, someone in which this is their skillset. If they have the time, and they're going to put the necessary energy and attention towards it, then you can have them edit it for you. Ensure that it's done right because once you release this book out into the world, this is pretty much a representation of who you are.

Number three, this is the option that I would recommend. This is the option that I chose to do for my last three books. Hire a professional at an affordable price. Use freelance sites like Upwork.com, Freelancer.com, etc. Once you do your research, you will be able to find great work at an affordable price. Whichever editor you decide to work with, make sure they're using the track changes, a format offered by Microsoft. It's an editing software that allows you to see

" You don't write because you want to say something, you write because you have something to say."

— *F. Scott Fitzgerald*

All of the changes that the editor has made to your manuscript. And then, you can read through your manuscript, and you can accept or decline the changes.

Different Types of Editors

Let's go through the different editors that I believe you're going to need for your books. I'm going to give you three that are great for nonfiction. The first editor is called a line editor. This is someone who is focused on reviewing and editing your book line by line. They're going through your manuscript line by line, ensuring that you're organized and that your thoughts are organized. Grammar is not necessarily the number one thing. You can find a line editor that focuses on grammar as well too, but they're going to mainly focus on the structure of your work, your word choice, your paragraph usage, et cetera. For all the editors I recommend, make sure they use the track changes software offered by Microsoft.

The second editor that I use is called a copy editor. A copy editor focuses on the rules. This is where the editors check for grammar, syntax, spelling, sentence structure, and any inconsistencies. Now, this is why I said at the beginning of the writing process that you shouldn't worry about trying to get everything completely right for your first draft. You just write, write, write, write, write. A copy editor is going to make sure that your grammar, syntax, and spelling are correct.

The last editor is a proofreader. This is the person who's going to go through everything. And they're similar to the copy editor as well, but now they're focused on looking at everything, the whole writing process in its entirety, looking at it from beginning to end. They're going to also look at the rules and if everything makes sense. So you want to make sure that you get a proofreader as your last step. They're going to read through it.

" *There's no greater agony than bearing an untold story inside of you.*"

— *Maya Angelou*

I was fortunate that when I got my book edited, my copy editor and my proofreader was the same person, and they spent a lot of time—they had my manuscript for about 10-15 days. Going through the manuscript, I was able to see the changes made because they shared it with track changes on, which gives you the ability to see the different changes they made, and I was able to say yay or nay. So, when we're talking about the editing phase, these are the three major editors. There are many more out there. It all depends on the type of book you're writing, but when we're talking about writing a nonfiction book. These are the three editors that I would recommend, and you can go to UpWork.com or similar websites and get all three of these at a very affordable cost. Still, make sure that you also pay attention to the reviews in addition to the costs for the service. So far, everybody I've worked with for my books has had 4.9 or 5 stars reviews, and I try to make sure they've worked with a lot of clients.

I don't like to see five stars as a rating, and they've worked with one client. I like to see five stars with at least 100 or more clients if possible. That's just a personal preference that I had because I want to make sure that they have the experience and the practice. You will want to make sure that you're focused on somebody that works on books. It's important for book editing. Having somebody who works on books will have a better understanding of the flow and how things should be structured. All right, so hopefully that's helpful for you as it relates to the editing process. Now that we've discussed the editing, let's go to formatting.

" Write what should not be forgotten."

— *Isabel Allende*

Formatting or Typesetting

Getting your book formatted is totally different from getting your book edited. Don't get your book formatted until your book has been edited because formatting is the absolute last stage as far as everything on the inside of the book before we get to the cover design and sending your book off to the publisher.

So when you send your manuscript to the individual that's going to do your formatting or typesetting, you have to make sure that all the spelling and grammar is correct and that all the titles have been corrected because your formatter is not responsible for correcting any errors, syntax or spelling. That is not their job. If you open a book from your bookshelf, you will notice that on each page, everything is centered. That you have a nice margin on the right, left, top, and bottom of the page. You will notice the page numbers and headings for each chapter. Notice the words are not bleeding over into the margins. The paragraphs are not on top of each other. The spacing looks very nice. That is what we call formatting or typesetting.

Before we get started, here are the recommendations I have. Make sure that while going through this book process, you find someone who can format your book for paperback version and for KDP, which is Kindle direct publishing, an **amazon.com** company. This will be the ebook version of your book. Your completed paperback manuscript will be formatted into a PDF. While your KDP version will be formatted in a Mobi file. If you decide to publish your paperback and ebooks through another platform, make sure to find out what files they require to upload your manuscript.

Additional Paperback and Ebook Platforms:
- Apple iBookstore
- Barnes and Noble Nook
- Google Play
- IngramSpark
- Smashwords

" It is only by writing, not dreaming about it, that we develop our own style."

— *P.D. James*

Formatting Options:

Here are a few options you have. Number one, you can do it yourself. Now, I would stay away from this completely unless you're somebody with this skillset. Number two, you can have a friend or family member format your book for you if this is a skillset for them. Number three, this is the best option, and this is what I recommend. Hire a professional at an affordable price. Again, you can go to Fiverr, Upwork, Freelancer.com, or you can find a local professional that will format your book.

Formatting Includes:

Title page
Copyright page
Table of contents
Introduction page
Dedication page
Acknowledgment Page
Page numbering
All pages in the book

Ensure to include all your front matters during this formatting process, that is, your table of content, which is your copyright page, your introduction, your dedication pages. Make sure that you or your freelancer will format your back matter, which is the authors about page, your index page or bibliography, or any other pages you want to put in your book. If you want to offer something to your clients, if you want to send them to your website, you can have that on a page, and then you can have a notes section as well.

Remember, you can do it yourself, you can get someone to help you with that or hire someone, which I recommend.

" Focus more on your desire than on your doubt, and the dream will take care of itself."

— *Mark Twain*

We talked about getting your voice transcription and your audio transcription. And then, we also talked about the different editors from line editor, copy editor as well as your proofreader. Lastly, the formatting. Make sure that you're getting your book formatted in paperback as well as the ebook version. Ensure that the person formatting your book gives you an affordable option to do the front matter as well as the back matter.

Once you have all of that, you literally have everything from A to Z to help you get the editing and the formatting process complete. If you need to, go back through this information. Take notes, make sure you apply everything we discussed. Find your team and get everything to them. And once you get it back, you are one step closer to having your book in your hands.

" It's none of their business that you have to learn to write. Let them think you were born that way."

— *Ernest Hemingway*

CHAPTER 6

⚜

BOOK COVER DESIGN

At the beginning of this book, we talked about the 10 questions that I wanted you to come up with that will help you with the writing process. If you had more than 10 questions, that's perfectly okay. I also talked about focusing on common words that came up as you formed those questions and while answering those questions. Now, we're going to be talking about designing a book cover, which is the front, the spine and the back of your book; we have to talk about your title.

Notice we haven't brought up the title yet, so let's discuss that. I'll use my book as an example. The title of one of my books is called Next Level Students Success. When I was doing my writing outline, I noticed the same theme kept coming up for me. Which was "Student Success." Since student success kept coming up, I decided to put that in my title because that's the intended audience for my book. So it's very important that in your book title, you are speaking to your audience and solving a problem. Students are my audience for this example but, helping them take their success to the next level is the problem I'm solving. Because my last two books were written for high school and college students, it's easy to put student success in my title. Once a potential buyer sees student success, they're going to realize, "Hey, I have students, and this is potentially a great book for my students." Even if students see it, if it says next-level student success, by being students, they may pick up the book and say, "Hey, I want to get more information about this topic."

" It doesn't matter how many book ideas you have if you can't finish writing your book."

— *Joe Bunting*

When you're coming up with your book title, I want you to think about a title that, number one, is going to speak to your audience. So if you're in a youth market, have something youth-related, success-related, student-related. If you're in the spiritual space, the faith space, the religious space, have something to speak to that. If you're in the marketing space, the sales space, the entrepreneurship space, have something in your title that will speak to that. This is very important. Make sure to select a title that's going to solve a problem. And then, with a subtitle, it gives added value. Notice my audience and the problem is identified in the title Next level Student Success. My subtitle is Practical Ways to Achieve Success in School and In Life. Simple. So that's just an extra added value. All right, so that's the front cover—this is something I want you to consider as it relates to your front cover wording.

Now that we have a title, it is time to design your book. I'm so excited. One of the easiest things I would suggest that you do is to go back to your home library or local library. You can also go online to Amazon for this activity. Look for books that stand out to you. Here's a suggestion or a hint. Publishers, major publishers, spend a lot of money in designing these books. They spend a lot of money on the psychology behind it, and they spent a lot of money on the colors behind it.

So, depending on what type of market you're getting into, I want you to really pay attention to that. After doing this exercise of looking at books that stood out to me, I started researching the colors of the covers. I chose to go with gray, dark orange, and light orange. If you look at the psychology of those colors, you will notice that they symbolize friendship. They symbolize confidence; they symbolize friendliness. So that's why I decided to pick those colors so that when individuals see my book cover, they see that yes, this guy is friendly, this guy is confident, and this guy is trustworthy. So that's the reason I chose those colors.

So when you're designing, I want you to pick a few books and ask yourself, are these going to be good in my genre?

" If I waited for perfection, I would never write a word."

— *Margaret Atwood*

I looked at a few books when I was designing my cover. I found a few I thought were amazing. So I sent my designer a picture of the books and said, "Hey, I don't want to copy it directly, but I want to use some of the color schemes, and I want it to be something similar to this." Use other books as inspiration, and then add your personal touch.

The same options apply when designing your book cover.

1. Do it yourself if this is your skillset
2. Have a friend or family member do it if this is their skillset
3. Hire a professional at an affordable cost (Recommended)

Cover Design Options:

- 99Designs.com
- Upwork.com
- Fiverr.com
- Canva.com

You can find a local professional or go online to one of the above suggestions or similar websites. The same thing applies as with editing and formatting. Ensure that whoever you decide to work with has great reviews and samples of their work to show you.

Tip: Make sure you know your trim size (book size) and the number of pages for your book. Your cover designer will need this information to make sure the book cover spine size is accurate. The more pages in your book, the more likely you will be able to have a nice-sized spine where you can write the title of your book and your name and picture.

" You can fix anything but a blank page."

— *Nora Roberts*

Book Cover Art Work

I decided to go with a big, bold picture of myself for credibility. If you would also like to put your picture on the cover, ask yourself if it will help you accomplish the goals for your book. If you're someone that's seeking credibility, expert status, or face recognition, then putting your picture on the front cover might be good for you. A simple and affordable way to get this picture is to hire a professional at a great cost or have a friend or family member take your picture using the latest smartphone, and that will be great to send to your designer. You can just find a very nice location. Use a well-lit room with a clear background. Send your pictures along with all of the wording for the front, the spine as well as the back. You send that over to the designer you found, and they will put it together for you and format it ready in a PDF file so you can upload it on your desired platform.

All right, just to recap before we move on, for the front, we have our title. Remember, you want to pick a title that solves a problem, but also pick a title that's speaking to your audience. Number two, subtitle. Make sure that your subtitle is added value that's going to support your main title so that when the buyers see that, they're going to say, "Hey, this is something I'm interested in." They're going to see the quality of the front cover. They're going to see the quality of the spine, which would make them turn to the back and want to read the back.

Now, going back to the outline, remember I said it's very important to know the difference between your reader and your buyer. Your buyer is going to go to the back of your book. They're going to read it and say, "Hmm, I think this is a great book for me." Here's a small sample as an example of what I put on the back of one of my student book.

" Get through a draft as quickly as possible."

— *Joshua Wolf Shenk*

Opening

"This book is a student's guide to achieve success in school and in life. A wealth of knowledge that every principal, teacher, professor, counselor, parent, and student life director would want their students to read."

Once my buyer read the back of this book, they're going to say this is something I want my students to read. After that compelling opening, I explain what they will get from the book.

Now, don't tell them everything they're going to get from the book. You're just going to tell them the outcomes they can expect if they implement what's in the book. I'll give you an example.

Outcomes

It says, "In next level, student success, Dennard shares practical, actionable tips that students can implement immediately to achieve success. If you want stronger personal relationships, to improve academically, to become an effective student leader, or increase your self-belief, this book will challenge you to do exactly that and more."

Now notice I listed what this book can do, but I never say how to do it. The how is in the book. Give them enough to make them say, you know what? This is a book I think I need to have, and I think I'm going to order this for me. And then once they get it, if they like it, they're going to order bulk copies for their students, for their staff, whoever your audience is.

That's why the outline process was so important because now you're going to write up a nice blurb on the back. The top portion is a blurb about your book (A compelling opening paragraph) and bullet points of the outcomes from reading your book. Immediately at the end of the section, give your buyers a call to action to buy your book.

" There is no real ending. It's just the place where you stop the story."

— *Frank Herbert*

Example: If you are ready to live your best life today, you need to buy this book.

The second portion is a blurb about yourself (Authors Bio). This is the time for you to brag about all of your qualities and your qualifications. Under your bio, you can add your contact information, company information, logo, publishing company, and website where your readers can find more information about you.

Tip: Make sure that your book has a barcode and ISBN on the back.

Resources:

myidentifiers.com
Amazon KDP

If you have quotes from individuals such as colleagues, principals or people who are authority figures in your particular field or celebrities, you can add those quotes to the back of your book for buyers to read.

Last thing I want to share with you, once you are done getting your book designed and you approve it, ask your book designer if they can give you a 3D image of your book cover. This will be useful as you start marketing and promoting your book. You can use your 3D image to market and promote your book on social media, press release, as well as share it with family and friends.

Enjoying this book?

The best way you can thank a fellow author is to leave a review on Amazon! (Pretty pretty please with cherries on top. You are Awesome!)

Chapter 7

⟨∽⟩

Preparing to Launch your Book

I am super excited because we are one step away from getting your book published. Before we do that, we must go through what's known as the book launch team or the pre-book launch process. Now, this is very important because moving forward from this point on, I will be discussing everything that's going to be very beneficial as it relates to using Amazon's (KDP), Kindle direct publishing platform to publish your book. In the next chapter, we will discuss publishing, and I'll give you different methods and suggestions. However, moving forward, everything you read from this point will benefit you using Amazon to publish a paperback book and Kindle version, which is Amazon's ebook. This method to launch your book can be used even if you decide to publish your book with another company instead of Amazon.

A launch team is essentially a group of people who supports you and have agreed to help make your book a success. From experience, I recommend that you start asking individuals via email, in person or by phone if they would be willing to help you with the launch of your book at least one to three months prior to your release. For those that agree to help, schedule a meeting with them as a group via phone, social media, or virtual. During this meeting, share the vision and goals you have for your book and find out if anyone has special skills or talents to make those goals a reality. Come up with a list of tasks for your team that would be beneficial to your book launch success and review with your team. You could also come up with ideas together while in your meeting. This is an amazing opportunity to get creative while bringing awareness and attention to your book.

" Be willing to write really badly."

— *Jennifer Egan*

Launch Team Task Suggestions

Each member share your book on their social media platforms

Each member share your book with someone personally

Each member purchase a copy of your book

Each member submit an honest, positive review about your book

Have a physical or virtual launch party

It's very important that you're able to create a team of supporters who are going to commit to purchasing your book and leaving an honest review on launch day. And what this is going to do is create what I call big Mo or momentum. The goal is to create as much momentum as possible on launch day that the algorithms in Amazon pick up and notice that you have a lot of activity. And with that, you're going to be able to move up in ranks for several different categories. I'll explain all of that moving forward. So number one, just keep in mind everything we're doing moving forward.

So the first thing we must do is create what's called a launch team. So what I would like for you to do is take out a sheet of paper and make a list of all of your family and friends that you can call for support to purchase your book. Now will be a great time while

" It is by sitting down to write every morning that one becomes a writer."

— *Gerald Brenan*

Your book is being formatted, while it's being edited, while the cover design is being finalized. This will be a great time to just pick up the phone and literally call the people on your list. I'm giving you the blueprint of what I did. I called every person on my list, one by one, and I explained to them that I was releasing a book. The goal of your phone call is to get a verbal yes, that on launch day, they will purchase your book and leave an honest review once they have read your book.

A great time to start marketing and reaching out to your launch team should be at least one to three months before your book is released. So from this point out, set a date when you would like to launch your book. When I started doing this exact process, I decided to set the date to launch my book as April 1st, so this process started about a month and a half prior to April 1st. As I called everyone on my list of family and friends, this was the first list I made. So I suggest you make a list of family and friends—we can call this your A list. You can give them an option to order your ebook, your paperback book, or both.

Now number two, I want you to have a B list. This is all of your coworkers and associates. You know people that are not necessarily your close friends and family, but you know them well enough that you feel comfortable to walk up to them and say, "I'll be releasing a book, and I was wondering if you would be willing to support me and buy the book on launch day. I will send you a link to Amazon, and you can purchase the book on the day it's released." By sending them a link via text or email on launch day, will make this process as easy as possible. The same thing applies as with list A; get a verbal yes from them as a supporter. Make a note or mark on your list to keep track of those who said they would support.

The major purpose for this is that it's our job to be intentional in creating momentum to get book sales. And to be honest with you, you can't wait until launch day to do all of this work. This is the planning phase. And if you do a great job planning, it's going to make your

" A professional writer is an amateur who didn't quit."

— *Richard Bach*

Launch day exciting, enjoyable, and you will be able to sit back and enjoy and watch as you climb in ranks.

So here's something I would like to share with you that I found out once my book was finally done. When you're getting your book edited and formatted and you get back your PDF version, you can email it to your launch team. Now you're probably saying, why is this important? Because on launch day, if you have individuals that purchase your book on launch day, especially the ebook version, they can immediately leave reviews. If you send them the book in advance to read, they will be able to leave a review immediately for your ebook on launch day. The reason that's so important is that if you can get individuals to purchase your book and leave reviews on day one, that's going to help the algorithms. That's going to help the momentum and help you move up the ranks. Now, this is something I found out at the last minute, and if I had known this, I would have climbed and reached number one much sooner. I'm trying to help you to make this process much easier than it was for me.

Use Social Media

Remember I mentioned getting that 3D image of your book cover. This is very important because while talking about your book to your launch team, you can also email or send them a text message showing them the book cover. This is going to get them excited and get them talking about your book.

Harness the power of social media. This is an amazing tool to launch your book. Instagram, Facebook, Twitter, LinkedIn, etc. If you have any of these social media platforms, this is a great chance for you to get people excited and start spreading the word before your book comes out. So what you're going to do is, in addition to having your launch team, you can put together a promotional thumbnail or a promotional picture to share with your followers that your book is coming soon. You can find someone on Fiverr to create this for you or do it yourself on Canva.com.

" You write to communicate to the hearts and minds of others what's burning inside you, and we edit to let the fire show through the smoke."

— *Arthur Plotnik*

CHAPTER 8

PUBLISHING

Now, as promised, I would share a few publishing companies that you may look into. However, I have not personally used them, so I will not give them my full recommendation, but I wanted to give you a few options if you would like to look into them.

booksjustbooks.com
lighteningsource.com
lulu.com

As mentioned prior, I will be focusing on using Amazon and the KDP platform for our publishing needs in this chapter. I believe Amazon's a great option to get started as a self-publishing author. I did not say the best, but a great place to start.

So you're probably saying, why are you so interested in using Amazon's platform? Well, here are a few reasons. First and foremost, it's an all-inclusive platform, meaning you can upload your book, have paperback books, eBooks (Kindle), or print on demand, meaning if you need just one book, you can have that one book printed and sent to a client, customer, or yourself, and that's a very good option. Back in the days, I remember ordering hundreds of books, having them sit at my house and selling them over time, those days are over. Next, Amazon is massive. Their platform, their infrastructure is massive. They're everywhere. They're worldwide. They have an infrastructure put in place, and they can ship your books all around the world. Number three, an amazing search engine. We know the big search engines such as YouTube and Google. Amazon is one of the major search engines today that individuals are going to, not only for

" So the writer who breeds more words than he needs, is making a chore for the reader who reads."

— *Dr. Seuss*

Books, but they're also going for other items. Number four, I think this is huge—the prime membership. You have a lot of members that have a prime membership, and because they have a prime membership, they can get your book shipped to them at no cost. That is huge. And then lastly, and I think this is one of the best reasons—you can get the best seller status using the Amazon platform, which will lend credibility to your name and credibility to you as an author.

So, I believe these are some major reasons why I think this is a great platform for you. And for the amount of money you will be paying Amazon to print your book and ship your book and handle all of the customer service, I think it's well worth it. So moving forward, we're going to be discussing everything relating to the Kindle direct publishing platform (KDP). With that said, I would like you to go to kdp.amazon.com, which is where we're going to set up your Amazon account. I'll walk you through all of the basics, but then everything else you would have to read on your own, and it's based on preference, but I'll give you all of the basic information you will need, and then I will give you some very, very important things to pay attention to. So number one, you're going to sign up for your Kindle direct publishing account.

The first thing you're going to do is just set up all of your personal information. If you currently already have an Amazon account, you can use the same login and password for your KDP, or if you would like to keep them separate, you can do that option as well. So first thing, we're going to set up an account, and before we can do anything else, they're going to ask for all of your personal information—name, address, phone number, and basic information. After they've asked for the basic information, they're going to ask for your bank account information. Now, this is very important because this is the account you will be receiving your royalty deposits.

After that, you will be asked some basic tax information and then directed to the KDP homepage. Once you're on the homepage, you're going to have two options. Would you like to start setting up your

" Let me live, love, and say it well in good
sentences."

— *Sylvia Plath*

Kindle version or would you like to start setting up your paperback book? If you're going to be doing both versions, paperback and Kindle, I recommend that you set up the paperback first. If you're just doing an ebook, then you can just go ahead and set up your ebook, but I recommend doing both so you can give your buyers multiple purchasing options.

Proofs

Once you have uploaded all of the required information for your book, you should order a proof of your book. Amazon will allow you to order up to five proofs at a time. This is a physical copy of your book with the ISBN covered and a strip on the front cover that reads "not for resale." So if you wanted to order a few proofs and send them out to people to proofread, you would have that option. I highly recommend that you take advantage of this option. This a great chance to see what your book will look like before it's published and ordered by your readers. This is also a chance to catch any last-minute errors or mistakes.

When I received my proof for my fourth book, I noticed that my picture that was supposed to be on the spine was bleeding onto my front cover. Thankfully, I ordered a proof and was able to make the necessary correction before I released my book.

If you don't need to make any changes and you are happy with your proof, the next step is to publish your book. So, really quick, let's do a review because this was a lot of information. Remember, you are going to set up your KDP account, and that's at kdp.amazon.com. They're going to ask you for all of your personal information. Once you set that up, they're going to ask you whether or not you want to start on your kindle or your paperback book. I recommend you start a new paperback book.

You fill out all of the information. Once you fill out all the information for the book, they're going to ask which categories you would like to list your book. Once you do that, you're going to start working on your cover. You're going to

" If you want to change the world, pick up your pen and write."

— *Martin Luther*

Upload your book cover and your manuscript. Next, you will approve it. Notice I said approve and not publish. Do not publish your book until you receive and review your proof. Once you receive your proof, if everything looks great, then you are ready to move to the next step, which is publishing. Your book will be available for order within 24-72 hours.

" No matter what people tell you, words and
ideas can change the world."

— *Robin Williams*

CHAPTER 9

eℐⱣ

10 GREAT WAYS TO LEVERAGE YOUR BOOK

Okay, your book has been published and sales are starting to pour in from family, friends, and others you shared your book with. Now what? This is the point where most people stop with their book. I recommend that you leverage your book to create more opportunities, in addition to your book sales. Opportunities such as more income, exposure, and credibility. Below, I've listed 10 great ways you can leverage your book. They are not in order of importance.

1. Build a business around your book.

Building a business around your book is an amazing way to leverage your book. You may be saying to yourself, I'm not a business person or don't have a clue of what type of business to build. Tip: Think in terms of what skills, knowledge, advice, or expertise that you have, and that is valuable. Someone or some company will gladly pay you for that knowledge or skill.

Here are a few businesses to consider.

Start a Coaching Business - Depending on the type of book you wrote, you will be able to offer coaching services to individuals. Examples of coaching services: Life Coaching, Career Coaching, Trading, Financial Coaching, Relationship Coaching, Business Coaching, Leadership Coaching, Entrepreneurship, Executive Coaching, Performance Coach.

Start Training Business - Managerial Training, Safety Training, Legal Training, Technical or Technology Training, Personal Fitness Training, Soft Skills Training.

Start a Consulting Business - Leadership/Team Building Consultant, Advertising Consulting, Marketing Consultant, Business Management Consultant, Efficiency Consultant, Environmental Consultant, Financial and Retirement Consulting, Risk Management Consulting.

2. Speaking Engagements

Become a public speaker. Okay, I know you are giving me a crazy look right now; however, let me plead my case. Public speaking is an amazing way to not only add an extra stream of income to your life but a great opportunity to make a huge impact in the lives of others.

If you're reading this book and you don't have any experience with public speaking or you are just terrified of standing in front of a crowd, I would recommend joining a local toastmasters club through Toastmasters International. Toastmasters International is a nonprofit educational organization that teaches public speaking and leadership skills through a worldwide network of clubs. You can get more information by visiting **www.toastmasters.org**.

If you are an intermediate or experienced speaker, I recommend researching and reaching out to local and national organizations that can benefit from your book. Specifically look for speaking opportunities, workshop proposals, or panel discussions. You can also contact an organization and express to them how your book can benefit their staff. Below are a few suggestions based on industries.

Student Leadership Organizations:

Future Business Leaders of America (FBLA)
Business Professionals of America (BPA)
Family, Career and Community Leaders of America (FCCLA)

Future Health Professionals (HOSA)
Boys & Girls Club of America

Professional Associations

Accounting Professional Associations
Animal Care Professional Associations
Association of Child Life Professionals
National Association for Family Child Care
Counseling Professional Associations & Organizations
Dental Professional Associations
Human Resources Professional Associations

Academia

Secondary Schools
Colleges
Universities

3. Host your own events

Another great way to leverage your book is to host your own local or virtual event. This could be done as a solo event, or you can partner with others in your network to host a successful event. Create an event that will offer an extreme value that people would be willing to pay for. You can hold your event at a local hotel, library, community center, church, restaurant, banquet hall, cruise ship, etc. Below are a few suggestions of events to host.

-Empowerment Conference
-Leadership Retreat
-Vision Board Party
-Men's Conference
-Women's Conference
-Couples Retreat

-Singles Retreat
-Family Conference
-Writing Workshop
-Entrepreneurship Workshop
-Business Conference
-Networking Event
-Team Building Events
-Public Speaking Training
-Wedding Planning Events
-Panel Session/Community Events
-Seminar (Select a special theme)

4. Create a course

Creating a course is not only a great way to leverage your book but also a great option to add an additional stream of income if done correctly. I recommend researching how to properly create a course to save you stress, time and money. You can package your skillset and knowledge in an online course that your clients can access via login. You can offer your course as a one-time purchase or monthly subscription. Find out which option will work best for you and your financial goals. Below are a few suggestions to consider as platforms to host your course.

-Thinkific
-Teachable
-Clickfunnels
-Kajabi
-Udemy

5. Generate Leads

Generating leads is an essential part of growing a business. Leveraging a book is a way to help generate those leads. According to the internet, "Lead generation is the initiation of consumer interest or inquiry into the products or services of a business." Leads can be created for purposes such as list building, e-newsletter list acquisition or sales leads, just to name a few.

A great strategy would be to offer a free e-book to potential clients in exchange for their contact information such as an email address, phone number, or even a mailing address. Now that you have the contact information for potential clients (if they got the free ebook), or a paid client (if they got the paperback book at a discount), you can market a much higher ticket service in the future. So here is an example of how it can potentially look. You can run a social media ad offering your book with a specific purpose and that can help someone achieve a certain outcome. You will receive their contact information in exchange for the ebook or paperback book. Over time, continue to build a relationship with your group of new potential clients by adding value to them in the form of newsletters or educational videos. Once you've delivered a good amount of free value, you can offer them a higher ticket product. This higher ticket product or service can be a course, workshop, coaching session, presentation, etc.

This same strategy could also work with your paperback book. You could offer the paperback book at a discounted price or even for free, with the client paying for the shipping of the book. Keep in mind that using your paperback book may have a higher perceived value to your clients but will require a much higher investment from you. I recommend starting small and studying marketing tactics, specifically for books.

6. Host Webinars

In the last example on generating leads, I shared that it's important to build relationships with your potential clients and add free value. Hosting free webinars is a great way to serve your audience while delivering extremely high perceived value.

In addition to offering free webinars to deliver value, you may also leverage your book by offering paid webinars. This is a great opportunity to offer exclusive service to clients while adding an additional stream of income. Examples of types of webinars to consider are Marketing, Health

Care, Business Coaching, Human Resource, Nutritionist, Fitness Coaching, Educational. Below are a few suggestions to consider as platforms to host your webinar.

1. Zoom
2. WebinarJam
3. GoToWebinar
4. Demio
5. EasyWebinar
6. YouTube

7. AudioBook

Converting your paperback book to an audiobook is not only a great way to leverage your book, but it is another potential option for a sale. With busy schedules and personal time being at a premium, many of your readers may want to listen to your book while working out, driving, flying on a plane, or while on a lunch break. The more versions you offer your readers, the better for both of you. Your readers will be happy, and you will be rewarded financially. Audiobook Creation Exchange (ACX) is a great platform to create your audiobook.

8. Merchandise and Products

Not only is this option fun, but you can also get as creative as you can think. Creating merchandise and products to compliment your book will give your readers multiple options to support you and your book while giving them something they want and/or need. Here are some great examples of merchandise and products you could offer.

-Bookmarks
-Stickers
-Magnets
-Buttons
-Pens
-Notepads

-Journals
-Devotionals
-T-Shirts
-Coffee Mugs
-Water Bottles
-Posters
-Tote Bags
-USB Drives
-Mouse Pads

These are just a few options to get your creative juices flowing. You can try one or a few of these or come up with one of your own.

9. Multiple Languages

Transcribing your book into multiple languages is a great option to leverage your book, and it's pretty simple to do. I decided to transcribe my fourth book to Spanish when I noticed people asked if I offered my book in Spanish. After hearing this request several times, a light went off in my head. I reach out to a few freelancers on Upwork and Fiverr. After reviewing profiles and explaining what I needed, my book was transcribed. I repeated the same process outlined in this book and was able to reach the Amazon Best Sellers List

10. Book Club, Masterminds, and Private Groups

The final option to leverage your book is to start a public or private group. This could be a book club, mastermind, or even a Facebook group. Creating a group will give you the opportunity to interact with and serve your readers directly. If you are promoting a new book or product, you can go directly to your group.

Having a private group is a great option if you want to add exclusivity. This will allow you to add an additional income stream through memberships and or monthly subscriptions.

Thank You!

I would personally like to thank you for investing your time in reading this book. My hope is that you apply this information for maximum results.

Your input is very valuable. If you received value from this book, please leave me a helpful review on Amazon, letting me and others know what you thought about this book.

Wishing you publishing success!

Dennard Mitchell

Resources

Copyrights

copyrights.gov
Official site to register your manuscript

Fiverr.com

*Book Edits / Proofreaders
*Book Formatting
*Cover Design
*Voice Transcription / audio transcription

Upwork.com

* Book Edits / Proofreaders
* Book Formatting
* Cover Design

Myidentifiers.com Bowker

* Barcode
* ISBN (International Standard Book Number)

Canva.com

* Design presentations, social media graphics,
* and more with thousands of beautiful layouts.

Remove.bg

* Remove image backgrounds for free. Good option if you don't have photoshop.

Self-Publishing Options to Consider:

kdp.amazon.com (ebook and print)
booksjustbooks.com (ebook)
Lighting Source: www.ingramcontent.com/publishers/print (all inclusive)
lulu.com

Trim Size: This refers to the dimensions of a document after it has been printed and cut down to its desired width and height from a larger sheet, prior to any folding.

- Fiction: 4.25 x 6.87, 5 x 8, 5.25 x 8, 5.5 x 8.5, 6 x 9.
- Children's: 7.5 x 7.5, 7 x 10, 10 x 8.
- Textbooks: 6 x 9, 7 x 10, 8.5 x 11.
- Non-fiction: 5.5 x 8.5, 6 x 9, 7 x 10"
- Memoir: 5.25 x 8, 5.5 x 8.5.

COMMON BOOK TERMS

Fiction: Fiction books contain a made-up story – one that did not actually happen in real life. These stories are derived from the imagination and creativity of the authors and are not based on facts. Example: The Alchemist by Paulo Coelho

Nonfiction: Non-fiction or nonfiction books are factual books. Unlike fiction books, they are based on facts and information that can be verified to be true. Example: How to Win Friends And Influence People by Dale Carnegie.

Trim Size: This refers to the dimensions of a document after it has been printed and cut down to its desired width and height from a larger sheet, prior to any folding.

Book Cover: book cover is any protective covering used to bind together the pages of a book.

Barcode: A barcode is the graphical representation of a book's ISBN and price. Barcodes are used on physical books, allowing them to be machine-read and facilitating automated sales and inventory tracking – a requirement for most large retailers.

Formatting: Formatting refers to the way you enter paragraph and line breaks, indents, spaces, typefaces and punctuation marks.

Book Spine: The Spine of a book refers to the outside edge of the book where the pages are gathered and bound. In addition to providing an anchor point for the pages, the spine provides the hinge action that allows the book's cover and pages to open and close.

Front Matter: When you open a book, the first page is not the beginning of your story. No book opens directly to 'Chapter 1'. You see a half-title and full title, a copyright page, a table of contents, acknowledgments, an introduction, and any other information you need to provide a reader before they dive into the main content. All of this is collectively called Front Matter.

Back Matter: Like the Front Matter, Back Matter is everything after your book's main content. Usually, this includes the About the Author, any sort of index or bibliography, and often a few blank pages.

Layout: The layout is the way your content appears on the page. Including the font, size, spacing, and justification of your text. Your image placement. The margins. The Header and Footer. Page numbers. There's a lot going on with the layout.

Title page: Announces the title, subtitle, author and publisher of the book. Other information that may be found on the title page can include the publisher's location, the year of publication, or descriptive text about the book, and illustrations are also common on title pages.

Copyright page: Usually the verso of the title page, this page carries the copyright notice, edition information, publication information, printing history, cataloging data, legal notices, and the book's ISBN or identification number. In addition, rows of numbers are sometimes printed at the bottom of the page to indicate the year and number of the printing. Credits for design, production, editing and illustration are also commonly listed on the copyright page.

Dedication: Not every book carries a dedication, but for those that do, it follows the copyright page.

Epigraph: An author may wish to include an epigraph—a quotation near the front of the book. The epigraph may also appear facing the Table of Contents or facing the first page of text. Epigraphs can also be used at the heads of each chapter.

Table of Contents: A table of contents appears at the front of the book and lists each chapter or section. Also known as the Contents page, this page lists all the major divisions of the book, including parts, if used, and chapters. Depending on the length of the book, a greater level of detail may be provided to help the reader navigate the book.

Preface: Written by the author, the Preface often tells how the book came into being and is often signed with the name, place and date, although this is not always the case.

Acknowledgments: The author expresses their gratitude for the help in the creation of the book.

Introduction: The author explains the purposes and the goals of the work and may also place the work in a context, as well as spell out the organization and scope of the book.

Conclusion: A summary of the salient arguments of the main work that attempts to give a sense of completeness to the work.

Appendix: A section at the back of a book that contains relevant "extra" materials that don't really fit anywhere else. Items that might go in an appendix include copies of original documents, letters, maps, family trees, graphics, or recommended reading lists.

Binding: This refers to how the pages and cover are put together. A few common types of binding include:

Perfect Binding:

Also known as a "soft cover book," a perfect-bound book features a durable (but flexible) cover and is held together with a heavy-duty adhesive. Most mass-market paperbacks (the paperbacks you find in bookstores or grocery stores) feature perfect binding.

Saddle Stitching:

This is a slightly misleading name because there's no actual stitching involved. Instead, pages and cover are folded and stapled along the crease. Magazines, booklets, and short manuals often feature saddle stitching. Saddle stitching is very inexpensive.

Hardcover:

As the name suggests, these books feature hard, sturdy covers made of cardboard, fabric, or even leather and are often wrapped in a protective dust jacket. Hardcover books tend to be pricier to print than other types of binding.

Spiral Binding:

An inexpensive option that features a plastic or wire coil. Because spiral-bound pages can lay perfectly flat, this is a great choice for more "interactive" publications like workbooks or guidebooks.

Draft: A draft is a working (as in, not final) version of a book. In most cases, a draft is a Word document. Drafts go through multiple rounds of editing and revisions before they become final.

Dust Jacket: The removable paper cover that protects a hardcover book. Most dust jackets have a cover illustration, a book synopsis on the front inside flap, and an "About the Author/About the Company" blurb on the back inside flap

Editing: Unlike proofreading, which focuses on small grammar and spelling errors, editing is all about the big picture. Editing typically includes rewriting sentences for clarity, deleting unnecessary paragraphs, rearranging sections of a chapter, or adding details to make your writing more interesting. You can edit your draft yourself, or hire an editor to help you improve your writing.

Foreword: A short introduction that appears at the beginning of the book. The book's author can write a foreword, but it's often written by someone else, such as an industry expert or a respected author.

Galley: This is a sample copy of the book once it's been through the layout and design stages. The galley copy provides a final opportunity to review or make changes before the book goes to print.

Matte Vs. Glossy: You'll most likely have to decide between these two options when you choose a book cover or dust jacket. A glossy finish is super-shiny and a tiny bit reflective. A matte finish is low-shine and typically non-reflective.

JPEG: Pronounced "jay-peg," a JPEG is a common format for compressing digital photos. If you plan to include photos in your book, you'll likely need to convert them to JPEG format. Working with older photos? No worries. You can use a scanner to convert them to digital.

ISBN: Short for the International Standard Book Number, the ISBN is the unique number and accompanying bar code assigned to all commercially published books. A book's ISBN contains a variety of information, including the country where the book was published, the publisher, edition, and more. The ISBN is also used by bookstores and libraries.

PDF: A PDF is another common digital file format. Unlike a bare-bones Word document, a PDF looks exactly like a printed page and will include design elements, graphics, custom fonts, and more.

Print On Demand: A type of publishing option where books are printed individually when they are ordered. This is an economical alternative to traditional publishing, which typically requires you to print a few hundred books at once.

Prologue: An introductory section that appears before the main book. In a non-fiction book, you can use a prologue to provide context or background information or explain your relationship to the subject matter. A prologue might be a short vignette that sets the scene for the main story in a fiction book. A prologue is written by the book's author.

Proof: In publishing lingo, "proof" means a pre-print sample of a book. Typically, your publisher or printer will provide you with a proof to review before your book is printed. This is your last opportunity to do a thorough review and catch any typos or formatting issues before your book goes to print.

Proofreading: Proofreading means going through a final draft to correct small issues such as missing punctuation, typos, or grammar and spelling errors.

Publisher Vs. Printer: What's the difference? In most cases, a publisher handles all aspects of your book, from layout and design to printing, sales, and distribution. (Depending on what kind of publisher you're using, a publisher may handle marketing and publicity, too.) A printer does exactly what the name suggests: They print your book. Printers don't normally offer additional services like graphics, design or marketing.

Self-Publishing: Self-publishing is an increasingly popular option, and with good reason: It's easy, it's faster than traditional publishing, and it's a great choice if you're writing for a smaller audience and/or you want to retain complete creative control over your book. As a self-publishing author, you must produce the final draft and supply the funds required to design, market, and distribute your book. You must also decide how many copies will be printed and pay for each one.

Traditional publishing: Traditional publishers take all the risks.

They pay for everything from editing, proofreading, typesetting, printing, binding, cover art and design, promotion, advertising, warehousing, shipping, billing, and paying author royalties.

EBook: Short for "electronic book." eBooks are an increasingly popular alternative to traditional publishing. eBooks look exactly like traditional books, but they are designed to be read on tablets or dedicated eReaders (like the Amazon Kindle or the Barnes & Noble Nook). Many self-published authors prefer eBooks because they are much less expensive to produce than traditional paper books.

KDP: Kindle Direct Publishing is used by authors and publishers to independently publish their books directly to the Kindle Store.

Mobi File: Mobi files are the ebook files used exclusively by Amazon's Kindle Store. Mobi file extension is used for storing eBooks.

Audio Transcription: Audio transcription is the notation in writing or symbols of a sound file of some sort, whether analogue or digital. It is usually used in the context of a recording of a human's voice or voices and is also used in the context of the business of transcription, which is to notate a sound recording and turn the sounds into words or words that describe sound effects.

Track changes is an editing command that is commonly used when you create an original document and make changes and want to keep track of the changes made to that original document.

Thank You!

I would personally like to thank you for investing your time in reading this book. My hope is that you apply this information for maximum results.

Your input is very valuable. If you received value from this book, please leave me a helpful review on Amazon, letting me and others know what you thought about this book.

Wishing you publishing success!

Dennard Mitchell

www.ingramcontent.com/pod-product-compliance
Lightning Source LLC
Chambersburg PA
CBHW070248290326
41930CB00042B/2930